BIBLE VERSES TO REMEMBER SER

GIVE GOD
YOUR WORRIES

SALLY MICHAEL

Illustrated by
SENGSAVANE CHOUNRAMANY

Dedicated to Lydia Cardozo.
May you know that Jesus cares for you
and trust him with all your heart.

New Growth Press, Greensboro, NC 27401
Text Copyright © 2023 by Sally Michael
Illustration Copyright © 2023 by Sengsavane Chounramany

All rights reserved. No part of this publication may be reproduced, stored in a retrieval system, or transmitted in any form by any means, electronic, mechanical, photocopy, recording, or otherwise, without the prior permission of the publisher, except as provided by USA copyright law.

Unless otherwise noted, Scripture quotations are from The ESV® Bible (The Holy Bible, English Standard Version®). ESV® Text Edition: 2016. Copyright © 2001 by Crossway, a publishing ministry of Good News Publishers. The ESV® text has been reproduced in cooperation with and by permission of Good News Publishers. Unauthorized reproduction of this publication is prohibited. All rights reserved.

Scripture quotations marked (NIV) are taken from the Holy Bible, New International Version®, NIV®. Copyright © 1973, 1978, 1984, 2011 by Biblica, Inc.™ Used by permission of Zondervan. All rights reserved worldwide. www.zondervan.com The "NIV" and "New International Version" are trademarks registered in the United States Patent and Trademark Office by Biblica, Inc.™

Cover/Interior Design and Typesetting: Dan Stelzer
Cover/Interior illustrations: Sengsavane Chounramany

ISBN: 978-1-64507-343-7
Library of Congress Control Number: 2023934676

Printed in India

30 29 28 27 26 25 24 23   1 2 3 4 5

CAST ALL YOUR ANXIETY ON HIM BECAUSE HE CARES FOR YOU.

1 PETER 5:7 NIV

Have you ever seen a bird build a barn to store food in?

Of course not. That would be silly! Birds don't plant seeds, wait for plants to grow, and then keep the food in barns like people do. They don't have to. Jesus tells us that God takes care of the birds.

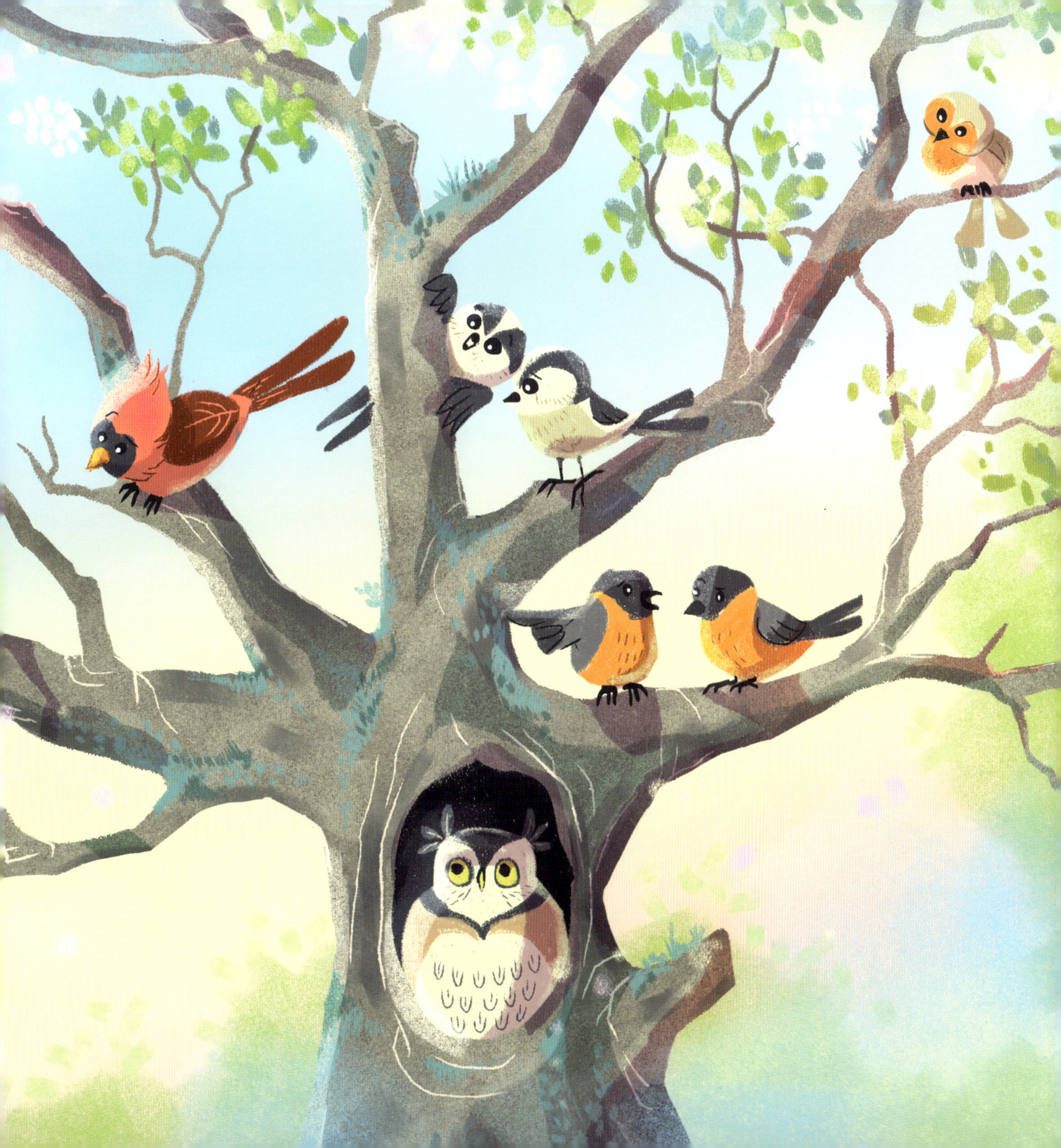

God gives birds bugs and seeds and berries and nuts to eat. They don't worry about breakfast, lunch, or dinner. They just eat what God has for them.

God takes care of birds . . .

and deer and lions,
and the sun and the moon,
the air and rain . . .

everything in his world.

And God takes care of you, too.

But do you sometimes worry about things?
Are you a little nervous about
what might happen or
what might not happen?

Do you ever think:
What if mommy forgets to pick me up after Sunday school?
Or, What if I get lost? Or, There are so many kids in this room.
It is too noisy for me. I'm not sure I want to be here.
Or, I don't want to be alone at night.

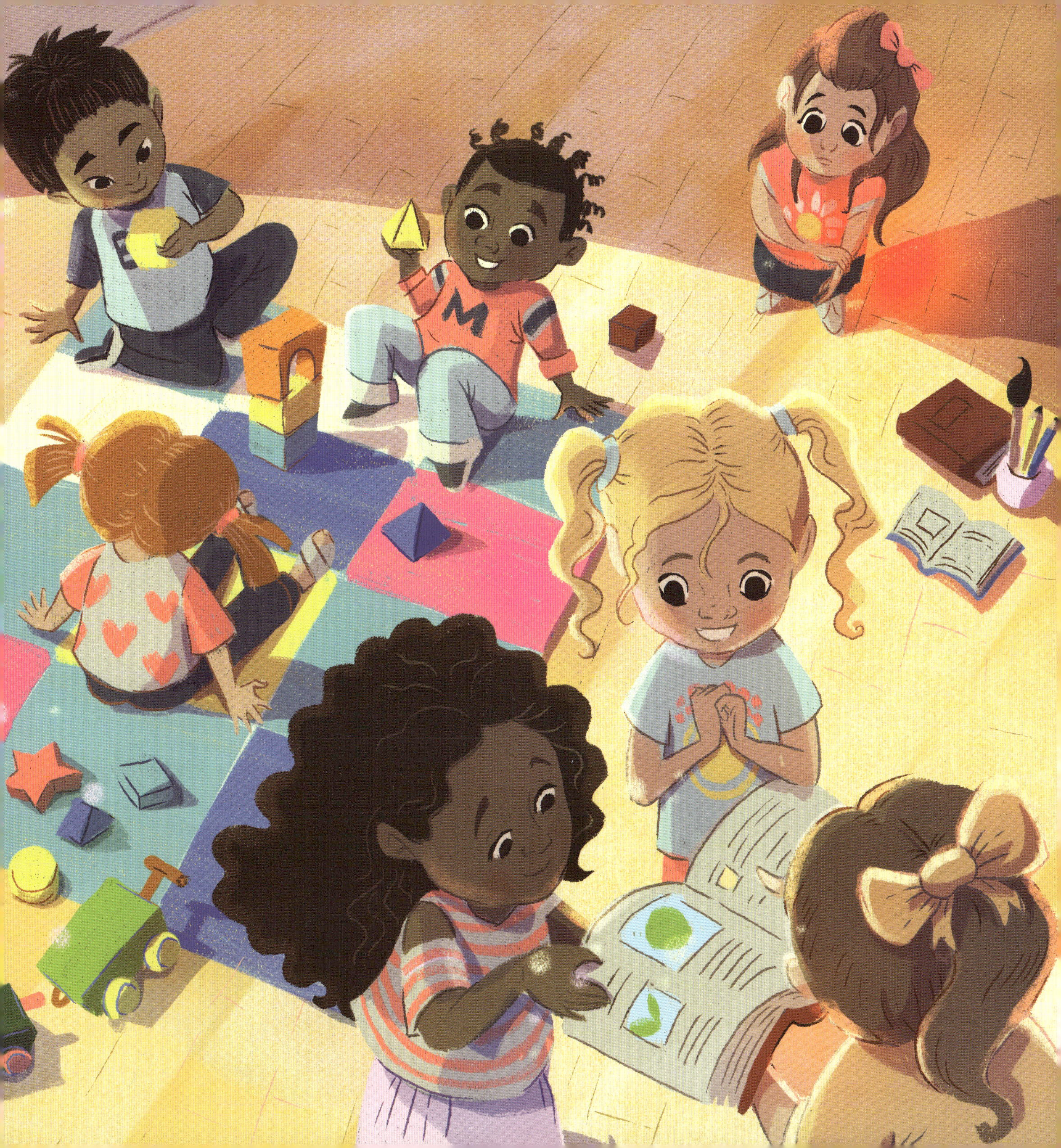

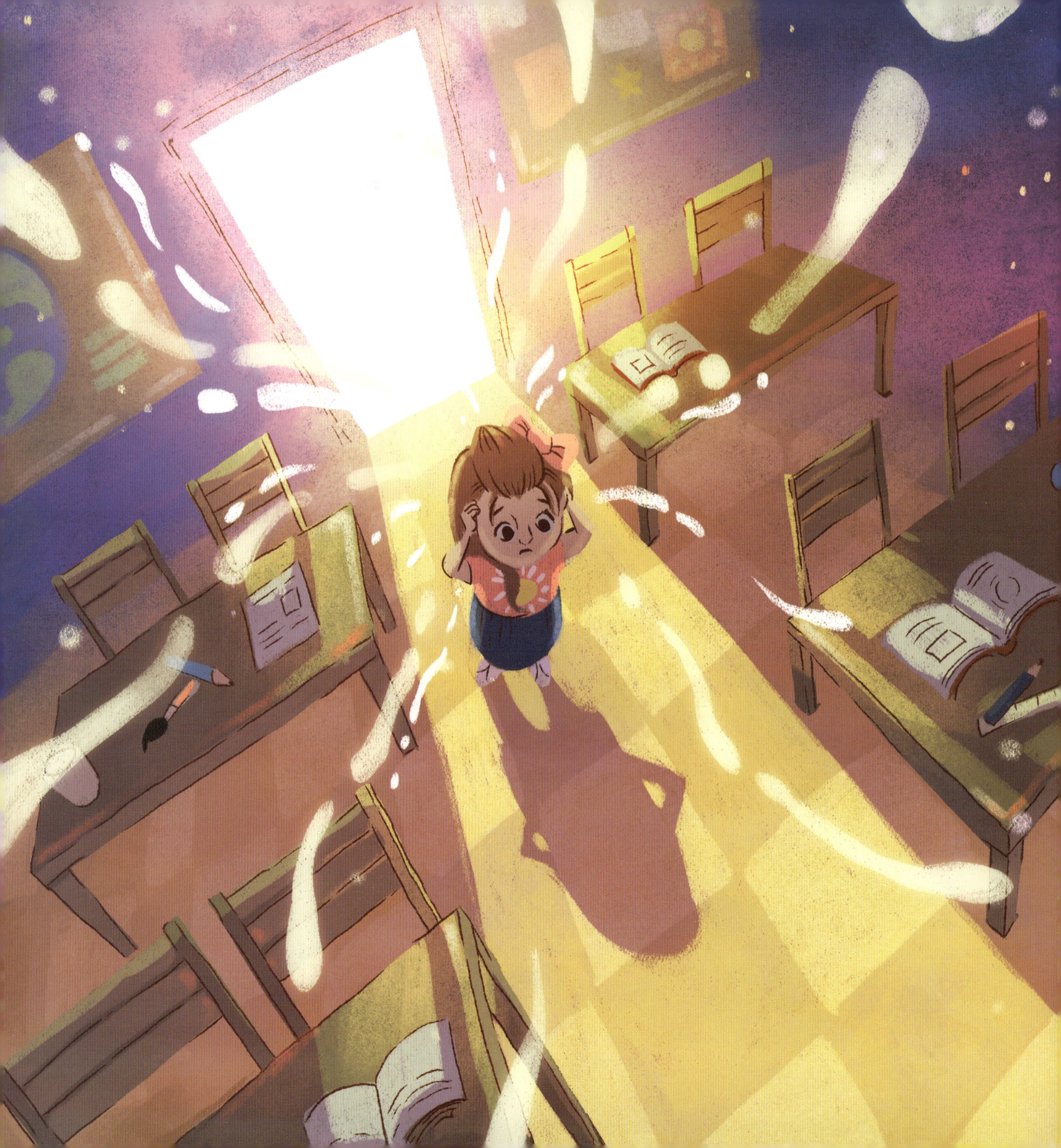

That is called having worry or anxiety.

It is a little like feeling scared, but it's not as strong a feeling as being scared. It is being not sure of things. It is wondering what might happen, or if things will be okay . . . and thinking about them over and over and over and over in your mind.

The Bible tells us that we don't have to feel that way. We can give away our worries! This is what the Bible says:

Cast all your anxiety on him because he cares for you.

1 Peter 5:7 NIV

Do you know what it means
to cast something? It means throw—
like when you throw a ball or throw a stone.

When you throw something, you get it away from you.
You might throw a ball to someone else. Or you might
throw a stone into a lake or a pond where it is gone
and doesn't come back to you.

That is what we are to do with our worries or our anxieties.
We just throw them far away from us!
Where do we throw them? Do we throw them into a lake or a pond?
Do we throw them into the garbage—or out the window?

No, our verse says:
Cast all your anxiety on him
because he cares for you.

Who is "he"? He is God.
If you can't see God, how can you cast or throw your anxieties on him?
You can't pick up those feelings in your hand and throw them.
But you can throw them out of your mind by giving them to God.

So when the thought comes to you, *Will Mommy remember to pick me up?* you stop and remember how big God is and that nothing is too hard for him.

Remember that God is good.

And then pray to Jesus, who is God the Son: "Jesus, thank you for taking care of little birds. I know you will take care of me, too. I am giving you this worry. Please take it away."

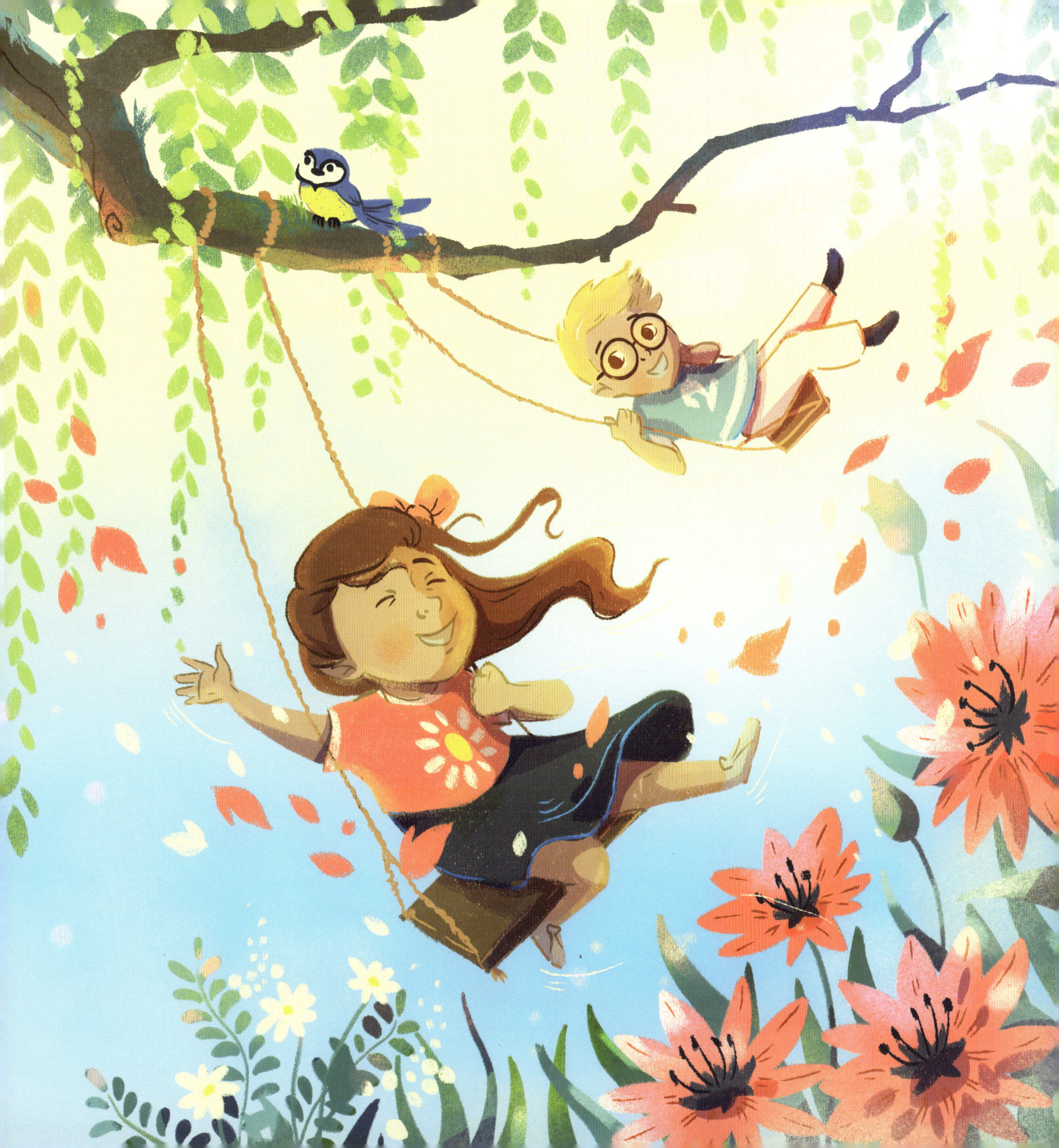

And every time you think anxious thoughts, remember that God is big and good. Then pray and give your worry to Jesus. Throw it away. Cast it on him. Do you know why you can do this? Because he cares for you.

Jesus wants to help you too.

Jesus loves children, and he loves to carry away all your feelings of anxiety.

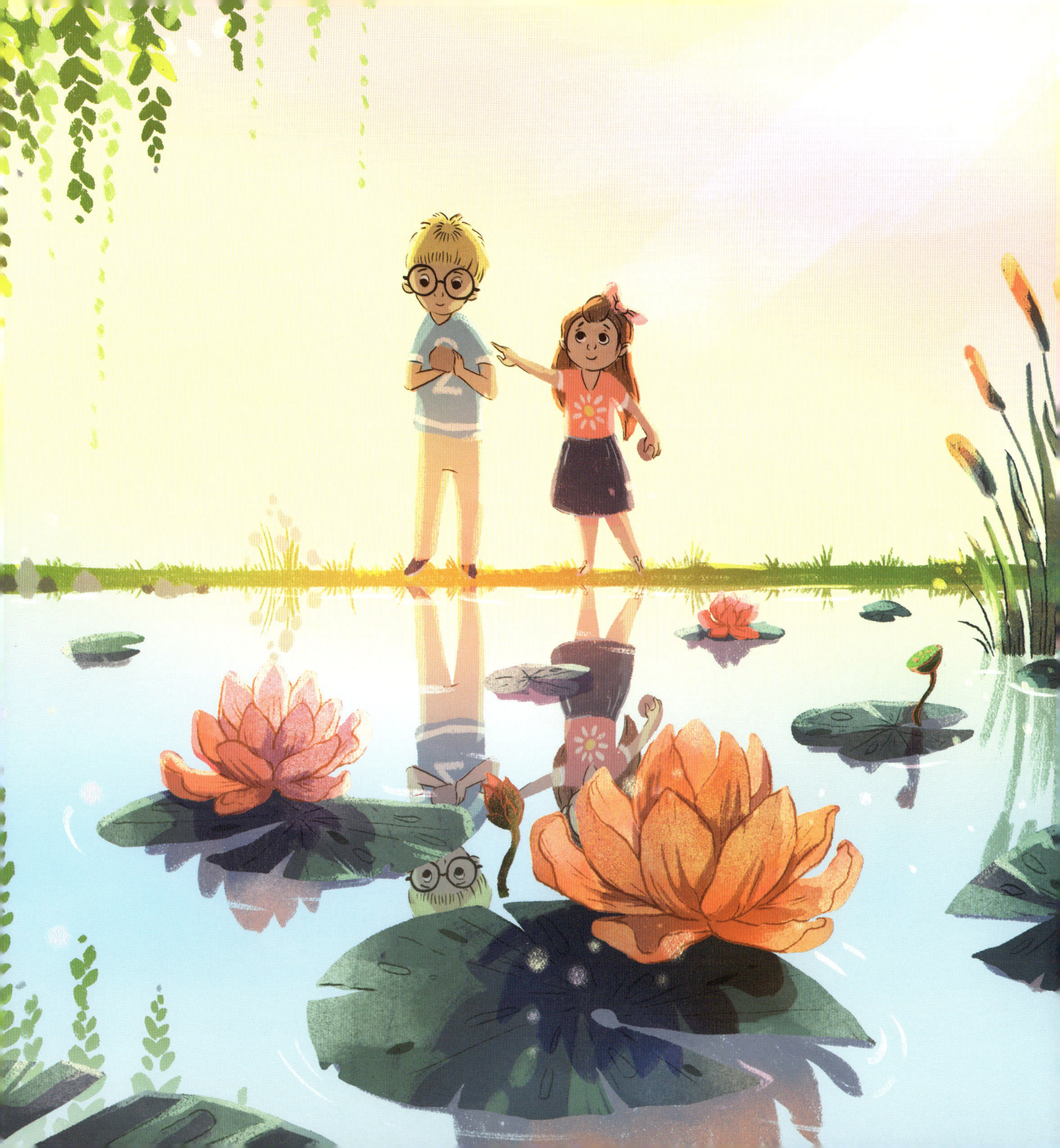

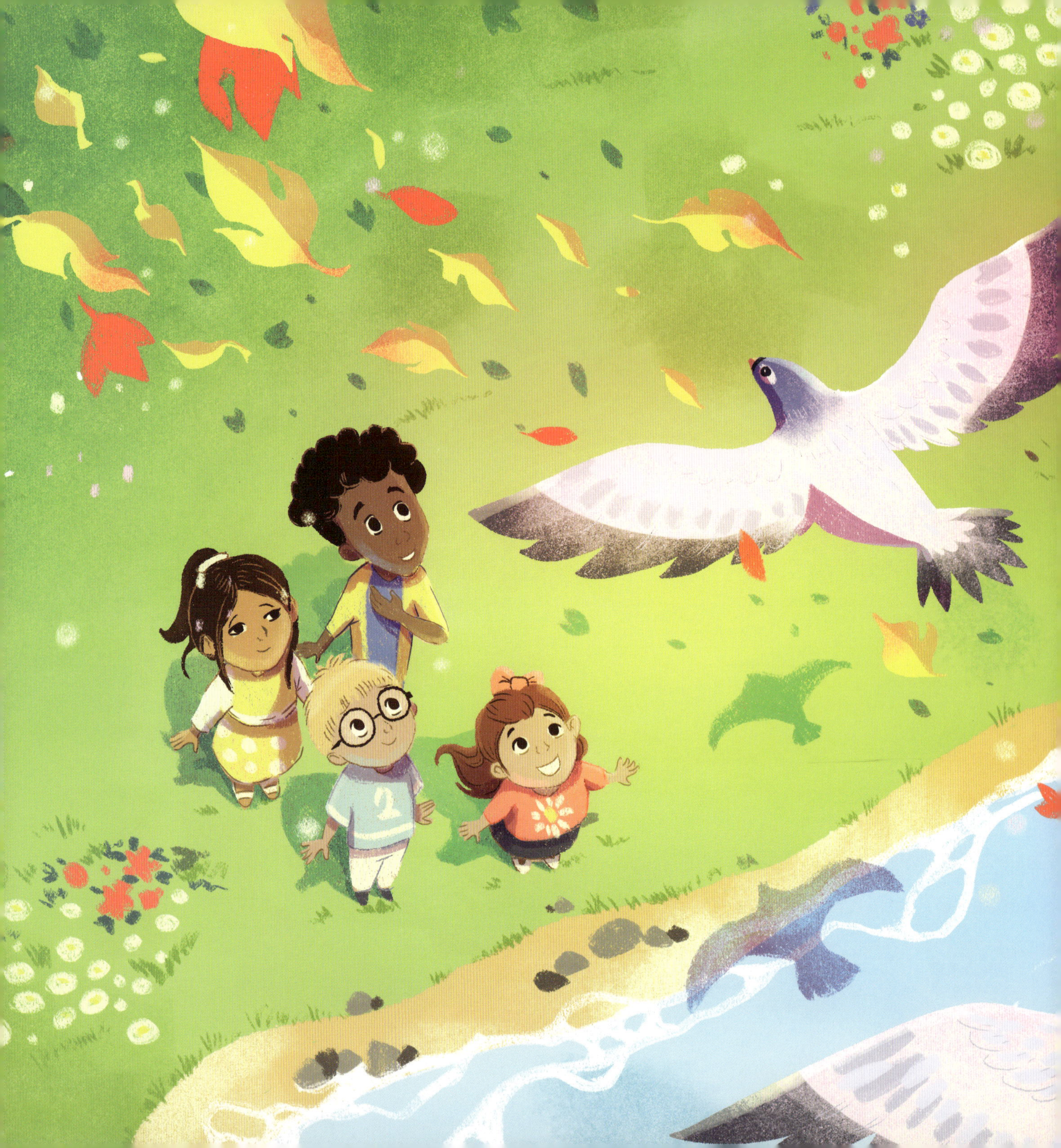

But will your worries really go away?

They will if you put your trust in Jesus and keep praying and casting them on him. They will if you trust him to be strong and to care for you. It doesn't mean they won't ever come back. But when they do, you will know just what to do:

Cast all your anxiety on him
because he cares for you.

PARENT NOTE

Children learn about God in baby steps—little steps of learning who he is, what he has done, and what he is doing now, plus little steps of obedience to his teaching and his ways. And, by God's grace, what they learn in little steps of trusting Jesus eventually grows into big steps of faith.

But children don't learn these things by themselves through their natural instincts. They learn them when they are taught the truths of God's Word. In Psalm 86:11, David humbly prays, "Teach me your way, O Lord." The ways of God are contrary to our sinful nature, which is why we must be taught by God (see also Proverbs 14:12 and Isaiah 55:8).

Teaching God's truth is necessary to lead children to obey the Lord from the heart. Children may obey God's commands simply because they like to please their parents or because it's expected of them. This can be a positive step, but it falls short of the kind of obedience that flows from personal conviction and love for God. Such conviction can only be brought about by teaching.

To come to saving faith, a child must embrace the whole of David's prayer in Psalm 86:11: "Teach me your way, O Lord, that I may walk in your truth; unite my heart to fear your name." Notice how he prays that the truth of God would affect his whole heart and life. Real, saving faith requires a change of heart. It requires embracing who God is and entrusting oneself completely to Jesus Christ.

God's Word can make your child "wise for salvation through faith in Christ Jesus" (2 Timothy 3:15). As you use God-breathed Scripture to teach, reprove, correct, and train your child in righteousness (2 Timothy 3:16), the Holy Spirit may chip away at your child's "heart of stone" and turn it into a "heart of flesh" (Ezekiel 36:26). Steps taken when little may lead your child to saving faith—to trusting in Jesus for the forgiveness of sin and the fulfillment of all his promises.

Your part as parent, grandparent, or other discipler of the next generation is to be a teacher, an example of walking in God's ways, and a model of a heart dedicated to God. May your prayer for yourself and your children each day be:

> Teach me your way, O Lord,
> that I may walk in your truth;
> unite my heart to fear your name.
> —Psalm 86:11

How to Use This Book

This book will encourage your child to trust Jesus and walk in his ways. The goal is to instruct their mind, engage their heart, and influence their will.

To Instruct the Mind
- Read the book several times.
- Explain any words or concepts unfamiliar to your child.
- Help your child to memorize the verse.

To Engage the Heart
- Interact with your child as you read the book. Dialogue about God and his ways. Help your child to see God's greatness and goodness. (See *Helping Children to Understand the Gospel* in the resource list.)
- Encourage your child to trust God in everyday events.
- Pray that your child would be receptive to the truth, trust Christ, and walk in his ways.
- Pray with your child that Jesus would give them a heart to love and glorify God.

To Influence the Will
- Talk with your child about ways to apply the verse in real-life situations.
- Encourage your child to act on what they have learned and to practice obedience to the truth.
- Guide your child in walking in the truth and living what they have learned.

Other Resources for Parents:

The Disciple-Making Parent: A Comprehensive Guidebook for Raising Your Children to Love and Follow Jesus by Chap Bettis

Gospel-Powered Parenting: How the Gospel Shapes and Transforms Parenting by William P. Farley

Helping Children to Understand the Gospel by Sally Michael, Jill Nelson, and Bud Burk

Instructing a Child's Heart by Tedd and Margy Tripp

Mothers, Disciplers of the Next Generation by Sally Michael

Teach Them Diligently: How to Use the Scriptures in Child Training by Lou Priolo

Tips for Helping Young Children Memorize Scripture

Memorizing by repetition works well when teaching verses to young children:

1. **Say the reference.** First, clearly pronounce the reference. Then ask the child to repeat the reference. (You may want to explain that a reference is like an address that tells where to find a verse in the Bible.)

2. **Repeat the verse in sections.** Say the passage in several bite-sized sections, repeating each section with the child.

    For example:
    a. Parent: *In the beginning*; Parent and child: *In the beginning*
    b. Parent: *God created*; Parent and child: *God created*
    c. Parent: *the heavens and the earth*; Parent and child: *the heavens and the earth*

3. **Repeat the reference.**

4. **Review the verse** several more times lengthening the sections each time, giving the reference before and after the passage.

5. **Discuss the verse.** After the passage is memorized (usually in 3-4 repetitions), it is good to dissect it. Explain the meaning of unfamiliar words. Rephrase the passage and talk about how the verse applies to life.

Memory Verse Resources:

"Foundation Verse Cards." Verse cards for 2- to 5-year-olds in ESV or NIV. Truth78. https://www.truth78.org/foundation-verses-resources.

"Foundation Verse Coloring Book." Truth78.org

Fighter Verses. App for Apple or Android (includes Foundation Verses)

LIVING BY THE WORD

What can you do to help remember that you can cast all your anxiety on Jesus?

Take a walk outside. Look at all the things God takes care of every day. Think about how big and how good God is.

Talk about when you are worried. Ask another person to help you pray and "cast your anxiety on Jesus." When worries come to you, think about throwing a ball to someone or throwing a rock into a pond. Remember that you can throw your worries onto Jesus. Pray and ask for his help.

Memorize 1 Peter 5:7: "Cast all your anxiety on him because he cares for you."

Pray this prayer every day: *"Teach me your way, O Lord, that I may walk in your truth; unite my heart to fear your name" (Psalm 86:11).* Pray that you will learn what the Bible says about God and his ways, that you will obey God's Word, and that God will give you a heart full of love for him.